JBIOG
GORMAN

6/02

Hermann, Spring
R.C. Gorman,
Navajo Artist

W9-AVL-877

DATE DUE

MENDHAM TWP LIBRARY

ON LINE

R.C. GORMAN

Navajo Artist

Spring Hermann

—Multicultural Junior Biographies—

Enslow Publishers, Inc.

40 Industrial Road	PO Box 38
Box 398	Aldershot
Berkeley Heights, NJ 07922	Hants GU12 6BP
USA	UK

http://www.enslow.com

Dedication: To Margo

Copyright ©1995 by Spring Hermann

All rights reserved.

No part of this book may be reproduced by any means
without the written permission of the publisher.

Library of Congress Cataloging-in-Publication Data

Hermann, Spring.
    R.C. Gorman: Navajo artist / Spring Hermann.
      p. cm. — (Multicultural junior biographies)
    Includes bibliographical references and index.
    Summary: Covers the life and work of the contemporary Navajo
artist R.C. Gorman, from his childhood days on an Arizona reservation
to his commercial success and the recognition of his
artistic achievments.
    ISBN 0-89490-638-0
    1. Gorman, R.C. (Rudolph Carl), 1931– —Juvenile literature.
2. Navajo artists—Biography—Juvenile literature. 3. Navajo
Indians—Biography—Juvenile literature. [1. Gorman, R. C.
(Rudolph Carl), 1931– . 2. Artists. 3. Navajo Indians—
Biography. 4. Indians of North America—Biography.] I. Title.
II. Series.
N6537.G66H47 1995
760'.092—dc20
[B]
                                      95-8807
                                       CIP
                                       AC

Printed in the United States of America

10 9 8 7 6 5 4 3

Illustration Credits: Courtesy of R.C. Gorman, pp. 6, 9, 16, 19, 20, 31, 42, 55, 62, 65, 71, 81, 84; "Going Home From a Navaho Trading Post, New Mexico", 1950, Copyright 1981, Laura Gilpin Collection, Amon Carter Museum, Fort Worth, Texas, p. 30; Photo by Ken Gallard, p. 45.

Cover Photos: Courtesy of R.C. Gorman

CONTENTS

FROM CHINLE
TO HARVARD

R udolph Carl Gorman stood in front of
Leveritt House. This was where students of
Harvard University lived. He looked around at the
big red brick buildings. He was used to the tan clay
buildings of his New Mexican town. Then he
smiled at the many students, teachers, and fans of
his artwork. They had come to honor him.

A Day at Harvard

Mr. Gorman is now known by his initials, R.C.
He is a full-blooded member of the Navajo tribe.

R.C. Gorman enjoys one of his favorite pastimes—dining out with friends—as he did when he spent the day at Harvard.

Teachers at Harvard invited him to come in May of 1986. They were giving him an award. The Navajo Nation, where Gorman was born and raised, is far from Harvard University. The tribe's homeland spreads over 15 million acres in Arizona and New Mexico. Harvard is the oldest university in America. It covers only a few acres. It stands beside the Charles River outside Boston, Massachusetts.

R.C. Gorman is a very busy artist. He works hard each day. He is a very popular artist, but to be honored by Harvard is special. So R.C. Gorman came to Harvard.

Soon the crowd went inside where lunch was served.[1] The president of the university watched. Dr. Allen Counter gave Gorman an award. He read these words: "To R.C. Gorman, the Humanitarian Award for his contributions to American art and intercultural relations."[2]

Gorman had won many awards for his drawings and paintings. But this award did not just honor him as an American artist. It meant that he had helped create better relations between Native Americans and other races.

Gorman was expected to say a few words. He never cared for making speeches, but he wanted to express his thanks. He said, "I am not sure I can *talk* art—I *do* it. I hope my work speaks its own language. . . ."[3]

The Navajo Way

He spoke about being a Navajo:

> We who are now called Native Americans lived for thousands of years on this continent without damaging the earth, as many from foreign cultures did not. For this I cast no stones. For I have now spent most of my life and earned my living in the world of 'other cultures'—but without leaving my own.[4]

Throughout that day, R.C. Gorman grinned and joked with people. They talked to him about his drawings of Native Americans. Gorman drew his people with their varied expressions. He drew them with their colorful blankets, pottery, plants, and he drew their landscape. His drawings helped others to better understand Native Americans.

People spoke about his kindness to students and artists. They praised him for helping young people. People commented on his silver and turquoise jewelry. They noticed his colorful cloth headband. He wore it to hold back his long, black hair. Gorman had lived and traveled outside his native area since the 1950s. So he took it all in stride.

Achieving His Goals

During his day at Harvard, R.C. Gorman thought about how far he had come throughout his life. He talked with many white, black, Asian, Hispanic, and Native-American students. He helped them understand the way he lived his life. Gorman had learned that if you love who you are and what you do, you can achieve anything. If you treat everyone—your family and friends,

R.C. Gorman's work has taken him a long way from the Navajo Nation where he spent his childhood. His work has even taken him as far as Vatican City in Rome.

your coworkers, and your customers—with respect . . . then they will respect you.

R.C. Gorman was once a little boy called Rudy. He had traveled a long way from his birthplace in the town of Chinle on the Arizona desert. His journey was still ongoing. But on that day at Harvard, he liked to think about its beginning. The road along Gorman's journey had taken many turns.

THE EARLY YEARS

Rudy Gorman was always drawing. People said Rudy could draw before he learned to read or count. He could always be found drawing his world. He drew outside with hunks of burnt wood, rocks, or sticks. When he was given paper, he drew with pencil.

One such drawing says: "Drawned [sic] by Rudy Gorman when 4 years old."[1] On it Rudy drew a hogan (a round house built of adobe-covered logs) with a chimney hole and smoke. He drew sheep pens by a small tree. Sheep graze nearby. He drew roosters and a goat with large horns. A prairie dog pops out of its burrow. Beside it Rudy drew his toy wagon. On the ground lies a woven blanket. He drew his cousin Elaine with her long hair and skirt. Elaine herds the sheep. He even drew himself. In the back, Rudy drew the outline of the mesa against the vast sky.

This drawing tells us much about the boy who would become the artist R.C. Gorman. It shows how he could draw the world in which he grew up. Even at age four, Rudy had a good eye.

The Young Artist

Rudy was the firstborn child of Adelle Brown and Carl Nelson Gorman. Adelle and Carl were a young Navajo couple from Chinle, Arizona. Both came from large families. Rudy had many loving grandparents, aunts, uncles, and cousins. After Carl Nelson's mother had raised her family, she passed away. So Rudy's grandfather, Nelson Gorman, remarried. He and his second wife, Elouise, had Eleanor, Sylvia, Amelia, Clarence, and Nelson. The youngest two were close enough to Rudy's age to be his playmates. Rudy played with the family's German shepherd dog Mickey and the pet cats. For an only child, Rudy was never alone.

Living in Chinle

Chinle was built where two huge canyons came together. Canyon de Chelly was to the southeast. Canyon del Muerto was to the northeast. Ancient tribes once lived in these canyons. Their walls of rock rose thousands of feet. When the rains fell, rivers flowed through them. There was no other town as far as the eye could see.

In tiny Chinle, in the 1930s, Rudy's parents lived in an old stone house near the Catholic church. Adelle's mother's family followed the Navajo tribal religion. But Adelle had become a Catholic when she was a student. She taught Rudy that faith. She got along well with the Catholic priests. They bought baked goods from her and let her use their outdoor water. Rudy and his relatives played on the front porch of the priest's house.

Carl's mother and her family had gone to the Presbyterian church. But Rudy felt no pull between the two religions. He often went back and forth for services. When one of the churches gave a big holiday party, *all* the Navajos attended.[2] Rudy looked forward to these gatherings at church.

The Reservation and Beyond

As a youngster, Rudy knew about the world beyond the reservation. He liked to listen to programs on the family's battery-powered radio. He especially liked the westerns. He went to the trading post and saw Hollywood movies shown in the school auditorium. He loved to watch automobiles and airplanes as they drove through Chinle or flew across the skies. He then drew pictures of them. He dreamed of someday riding or flying in them.

The Navajos called their land "the Navajo Nation." The reservation was part of Arizona and New Mexico. The Navajo tribe had its own leaders and police. Rudy's grandfather, John Brown, was one of the early tribal policemen. The tribe also had its own language. It was a difficult one. Rudy learned both Navajo and English growing up. He spoke Navajo with his older relatives and friends. He used English at home with his parents and with the white people of Chinle. He easily moved back and forth between the languages.

Family Stories

Rudy would sometimes listen to his mother tell stories. One of his favorites was about his mother's grandmother. When Rudy was born, his great-grandmother arrived to help. She was a stern Navajo lady who walked with a cane. When she got to Chinle, she found that Adelle had to have her baby before it was due. Rudy was quite small and sickly. The white doctor at Chinle Hospital put him in a machine to keep him warm. Rudy's great-grandmother announced to Adelle, "Those crazy white people are killing your child!"[3] She waved her cane and caused a great fuss. The hospital staff let her take Rudy home. There she nursed him with bottles of goat's milk mixed with black coffee! Soon Rudy became chubby and healthy.

Childhood Games

As Rudy grew, he learned to race with the other children. He rode ponies and chased the dogs and lambs. The boys played games and swam in the streams. When he had the chance, though, Rudy would stop and draw.

Rudy's father thought that his boy took after his grandfather. This man, called Peshlakai Atsidi, made jewelry out of silver. Carl's mother, Alice, wove beautiful rugs. Rudy's father did not talk about his *own* love for art. There was no time for hobbies with a growing family. Rudy's mother knew the women on her side were also talented weavers. Creativity ran in Rudy's blood.[4]

This image is called "Striped Blanket." Gorman drew it first, then it was enameled and fired onto this vase. Many women in his family were talented weavers of rugs and blankets.

Troubled Times

Everyone had to work hard to keep the family going. The United States was in trouble at the time. People could not find jobs. The crops were poor. A dollar did not buy much. Many children did not have enough to eat. Rudy was a child during the 1930s, the time of the Great Depression.

Carl held several jobs to feed his family. He traveled the reservation. He herded, dipped, and butchered sheep. He also hauled coal in his old truck. The government schools bought the coal from him. He had to be gone much of time. Adelle worked as a cook for the Chinle Hospital. Relatives helped look after Rudy. Soon he learned to cook himself.

Rudy's chores included hauling the water from outdoors and chopping wood for the stove. All Navajo children did chores. He never complained. While he worked, he imagined better times. Not only did Rudy like to draw, he also liked to dream.[5]

The Sheep Ranch

During the summer that Rudy turned six years old, he spent time on a sheep ranch. It belonged to his mother's mother. There she had her summer hogan. Grandmother thought it was fine that Rudy was able to speak English so well. She, however, spoke only Navajo. She knew The People's word for all things.

"What is that plant called?" Rudy would ask. His grandmother would tell him the name. She knew if the plant could be used in a soothing tea or as an herb in cooking stew. She might use it for soap, or to heal a wound. "But why should we only use the plant that way?" Rudy would ask her.

"Because that is the way it's done," Grandmother would answer.[6]

Some plants could kill you and some were good only for Holy People who knew the special ceremony. To prove her point, Grandmother, who prayed in the Navajo way, picked a special lily. The plant could make you sick if you were not prepared in the holy way to receive it. She drank the nectar. Rudy watched her in awe, and he never touched the lily.

At sunset, Rudy would ask his grandmother: "What name do you give those stars?"[7] For each group of stars there was a Navajo name and a story. Grandmother would teach the stories to Rudy.

They sat in front of Grandmother's summer hogan listening to the night breeze. Rudy thought of all Grandmother had told him. He learned why the hogan door faced east. That was the home of the rising sun. The sun gave life. Grandmother taught Rudy so many things. He would never forget his people.

Art from Nature

After swimming with his male cousins, Rudy would sit in the mud. He would make cars and animals out of the clay. When his mud cars dried, they became his toys.

When Gorman was a young boy, he made toy cars out of clay. As an adult, however, Gorman began to sculpt different sorts of things. Gorman finished the clay model for his sculpture now called "Amelia." He had made the original sketches from a live model. In this picture, he is sculpturing her face and hair.

The Tribe

Rudy's family was not rich, but they belonged to a strong tribe. The Navajos encouraged their children. Rudy's relatives taught him history and culture in two languages. They gave him a love of design and beauty. Some summers his family

Here is the completed clay model for "Amelia." Now "Amelia" has been cast in bronze. A special studio in San Francisco usually produces Gorman's bronze sculptures. Only seven to ten are made from each model.

traveled to Gallup, New Mexico. There he saw many tribal dances at the Inter-tribal Ceremonial. His parents shared with Rudy the faith of the Catholics and the Presbyterians. These were their gifts to him.

During 1937, some changes came into Rudy's life. His brother Donald was born. Just when

Rudy got used to playing the big brother, it was time for him to start school.

Starting School

Rudy had two choices. He could go to the government boarding school. There he would be in class with only Navajo children. They all lived so far away that they stayed there all the time. But the Gorman house was within walking distance of the Chinle Public School. This school was a one-room school with a woodstove. Rudy could study there with the local white children. Some other Native-American and Hispanic students went there too. Classes would be taught in English.

Adelle wanted her son taught in English. She told Rudy, "You are going to the public school."[8]

Like most children, Rudy was a little worried about going off to spend his day in a strange place.[9]

He wondered if they would have books there. Chinle had no public library. The only books he was used to seeing were in church. He knew it would be nice to have them.

Rudy had a few days of sadness when he first started school. He had to get used to it. Finally, he decided school was a great place to be. The books were fun, reading was easy, and he made new friends. But the best part came when the teacher got out the crayons and colored paper. The teacher had all the colors of the Navajo world. Now Rudy had them in his hands.

3

GROWING UP

Rudy Gorman learned to read and write well at public school, but he liked art period best. When he was given modeling clay, or pencils and crayons, he was happiest. Everything he saw in the world or in his dreams was a good subject. Often he brought his drawings of pretty ladies home to his mother.

His teacher, Mrs. Shangkula, was kept busy at school, for grades one through six all sat in one room around the woodstove. Often she did not get to check her students' art work until they were finished. One day, she stopped and stared. She asked Rudy what he had drawn.

Drawing What Comes Naturally

He replied that he had drawn a lady. But this time Mrs. Shangkula was not pleased to see Rudy's drawing, for this lady was drawn with no clothes on![1]

Rudy had a feeling he might get into trouble for that. Once his grandmother scolded him for drawing nude figures on rocks up at her sheep camp.[2] He did not see why The People were so strict about keeping clothes on. The human body was interesting to him.[3] It was a natural and wonderful thing to draw.

Mrs. Shangkula gave Rudy a spanking, and sent him home with his drawing. Rudy's mother saw this drawing of the lady without her clothes, and found that Rudy had been punished. She knew that in school, if you disobeyed when you got older, the punishments got worse. So she turned Rudy around and gave him a quick spanking herself to teach him a lesson.[4]

Rudy became a very good student. His school did not have a lot of books. The ones Rudy read showed him a diverse country beyond the Navajo reservation. It was full of many kinds of people. Rudy studied with classmates from the Navajo, white, and Mexican-American communities.

Life at Home

At home, Rudy continued with his chores. He chopped the wood for the stove. He became a big help in looking after his little brother Don. Often, his mother had to work. Then, in 1939, when Don was two, a baby sister was born. She was named Donna. To Rudy, she was like a beautiful doll. He loved to play with her. As she grew, he pulled her in his wagon and took her for little walks.[5]

Once, when his father was home, Rudy got a boxing lesson from Carl. Carl was an expert boxer. Rudy was a good runner, swimmer, and rider. But he was not coordinated enough for boxing. After only one lesson, Carl gave up. Rudy was not sports-minded.

Carl and Rudy Go to Work

In the summer of 1941, Carl Gorman found a job branding cattle and dipping sheep in chemicals. The job was far northwest of Chinle at Kaibito. The job would be hard, hot work, but it paid well. Carl decided he wanted to take Rudy with him for the summer.[6]

Adelle agreed, telling Rudy to pay attention

to what his father told him. He needed to see what a man had to do to get along.

Rudy would miss herding sheep with his grandmother and playing with his relatives. He would miss his brother and sister. But spending a summer camping out with his father and the men would be exciting. Carl told him that he could help brand the cattle and hold the sheep. Also, Carl would buy Rudy drawing tablets and pencils.

Camping Out

Rudy and Carl went to Kaibito. Rudy went out in the field with his father and the men. He found that his father had a surprise for him. It was an old bicycle. Rudy was tall and strong for his age. He rode the bike everywhere. At the camp, young girls cooked for the workers. Rudy asked a girl to pose for him. He drew portraits of her. The men who worked with Carl were amazed that a little boy could draw so well. One of the government workers, a white man, told Carl: "That boy is terrific. I tell you he's going to be a great artist." Carl smiled to hear what he already believed in his heart.[7]

Each day Rudy tried to help with the cattle.

Sometimes his father faced danger in the corral. He was always in control, though. Rudy thought about the western movies with actors dressed up like cowboys. None of them was as good as his father. His father was a real cowboy.

Every evening Carl and Rudy ate together. They sat around a campfire. They talked about the Navajo way to do things. They also talked about the big, wide world. A lot of people were still hungry and without work.

Talk of War

Rudy heard his father and the other men talk about being soldiers, sailors, or pilots. He heard them speak about the war. Fighting was going on between countries across the ocean. This was confusing but fascinating for Rudy. When they had their dinners together, Rudy's father tried to tell him why he worked for the government. He explained that because he could speak English so well, along with Navajo, he helped the white people to talk to their people. Rudy understood that fathers had to come and go to make a living.

Carl was working in a stock reduction program. The government wanted to take away sheep, cattle, and horses from the Navajo to preserve the rangeland. They promised to pay the Navajo people. Carl wanted to see that promises were kept. These were hard times for all.[8] Rudy was ten years old that July. He was glad his father talked to him like he was a young man. He wanted to get a good job someday. However, when his father asked what he might like to do, all he could think to himself was how much he liked to draw.

Navajos Needed by Marines

During December of 1941, Japan attacked American naval bases in Hawaii. America then declared war on Japan. Carl Gorman had been working in the Arizona mountains with the stock reduction program. He was playing cards one night during the winter of 1942. The Navajo Tribal Chairman's voice came over the short-wave radio. He asked for Navajo men who could speak English well to come forward. They would join a special group within the Marine Corp.

Carl Gorman was the perfect man for the job. The age limit was set at thirty-five. Carl had turned thirty-six. He did not let that stop him.

He went to Fort Defiance, changed the birth date on his records, and enlisted in the Marines.[9]

Serving His Country

The Gorman children were proud that their father was going to serve their country. Only Rudy was old enough to sense a problem between his mother and father, but it wasn't his place to ask. After Carl left that winter, Adelle packed the family's clothes and things. She told the children she had been offered work that paid pretty well. They had to move to where the job was, near Flagstaff.

Moving On

Rudy learned in school that Flagstaff was outside the Navajo reservation. The job, his mother explained, was at the government ordnance at Bellemont. This was a place where the Army made and stored weapons. Many of the Navajos and Hopis were going to get work there to support the war. Rudy's mother also had relatives and friends who were on their way to Bellemont.[10]

Rudy, along with Don and Donna, left the only

home he had ever known. They all said goodbye to their neighbors and the priests at the church. The Army piled the Gorman family, along with other Navajo families, into troop trucks. They were driven out of Chinle. The winter wind howled and the family huddled together. Soon they drove onto the Hopi Reservation. It was located in the middle of the Navajo nation. Rudy had seldom been so far from home. Traveling was thrilling but scary. The trucks

Laura Gilpin took this photograph "Going Home from a Navaho Trading Post, New Mexico." Ms. Gilpin took pictures of the Navajo people from the 1930s through the 1950s. She saw the same image of women on the desert that Rudy Gorman had seen many times.

then stopped. They were picking up some Hopis who would also work at the ordnance.

In the lithograph "Desert Women," 1976, Editions Press, there is an image similar to Ms. Gilpin's photograph that Gorman has drawn from his childhood memories. In it, three Navajo women walk on the desert mesa. They look into the far horizon.

The Trading Post

Everyone was brought into the Hopi trading post. This was a store where people brought their goods and crafts. They traded them for groceries and supplies. The traders would sell these crafts to dealers off the reservation. The traders made a profit, which allowed them to bring back more groceries. This trading post had something Rudy had not seen before: oil paintings.

While Rudy's mother was busy with Don and Donna, Rudy could only stare at these paintings. Their Catholic church, where he had been an altar boy, had pretty windows and images of saints, but nothing like these amazing paintings. How could someone make such a beautiful picture of the canyons and the sky? What did they use? Someday he would paint like this. Finally, his mother pulled him away from the amazing sight.

They returned to the trucks and continued on their way. But Rudy kept thinking about those paintings. A Hopi must have done them. Who taught him? Who gave him the paints? Years passed before he discovered his answer.

A New Place to Live

The ordnance at Bellemont was an unusual place to live. Rudy discovered that The People were herded and fenced here. Mother explained that this was a special place full of weapons needed for the war. Fences were to keep bad people out.

Still, Rudy had always run free. Being fenced in was strange. The barracks were cold. The toilets and showers were outdoors. They couldn't buy foods they were used to having at home, such as lamb. Often, they had to eat antelope.[11]

Rudy and his family got used to life at the ordnance. Adelle got a job as a cook and a teacher's aide. She worked in the nursery school where Don and Donna went. There were always plenty of other children to play games. The Navajo camp was separate from the Hopi camp, but they got together for dances and movies.[12]

A bus arrived each day for the older children. It drove them to a public school in Flagstaff. In this new school, the teachers were very strict with the pupils. Children were told what to draw and paint. Rudy behaved himself, but he drew what he wanted to anyway.

During 1942, Adelle kept working at the ordnance. The Gorman family listened to the war news. Carl was in it somewhere. Many battles were going on against the Japanese in the South Pacific. Carl and other Navajos were on an important secret mission. No one at home knew what they were doing.

In November, new barracks were built at the

ordnance. A high, wired fence was put around them. During that winter, truckloads of foreign white men came. These new men spoke a language Rudy had never heard before.

Prisoners of War

Rudy found out these men were German prisoners! They had been captured by the American, the British, and the French forces. America was now fighting Germany. There were very few safe places to keep German prisoners in Europe. That was why they were being quietly shipped to America.

The Navajos got used to the German prisoners. Adelle told her children that these soldiers were just boys. Maybe they were the enemy, but they were stuck in the middle of a strange land. They were to be treated like human beings.[13] Rudy tried to talk with the ones who knew a little English. He even showed them pictures of the battles in *Life* magazine.

Adelle and the Gorman children lived with the prisoners throughout 1943. Rudy finished sixth grade. He had not seen his father for two years. Don and Donna were so young, they could hardly remember their father. Things had changed in Adelle Gorman's life. She had met a man. She got along better with this man than she had with Rudy's father. Also, she had to make a decision about where Rudy would go to school.

Boarding School

Rudy's mother told him about a boarding school past Chinle on the way to Gallup. It was called St. Michael's School. Catholic priests and nuns ran it for Navajo children. Rudy's mother thought he would get a good, strict education there.

Rudy did not question his mother. Most Navajo children went away to boarding school at a younger age than he was. His mother had taught him to be independent and to stand up for himself. Now it was time for him to show he was ready.[14] Rudy wondered if his father would ever come back home.

Rudy's mother did not know the danger the Navajo Marines faced as they carried out their secret mission. She did not know that her husband had a tropical fever, but kept fighting.[15] She could only tell Rudy that she thought his father would return. But when he did, things between Rudy's parents would never be the same.

LEARNING
ABOUT THE
WORLD OF ART

St. Michael's Mission School was built on a remote piece of land. It sat on the Arizona-New Mexico border. Franciscan priests ran the school. They had strict goals for their Navajo students. They wanted to educate them in the white man's way.[1]

Only English is Spoken Here

Speaking Navajo was against the rules. Rudy was used to speaking English in his public school classes, but before, he was allowed to speak Navajo when playing with the other children.

Many of the St. Michael's pupils spoke English poorly. Yet all had to do it.

Every morning at dawn, the pupils were sent to Catholic Mass. They then did a half day of labor in the fields and barns. Rudy wished he could spend more time in class.

The boys at St. Michael's had to wear dress shirts and neckties to class. Rudy's mother couldn't afford these shirts and ties. There was another hard rule. A boy was never to speak to a girl, even if the girl was your own relative! Punishments for breaking rules meant more work, often shoveling coal.

Hunger Pains

Rudy was always hungry. He was growing a lot that year. The school was very poor then. Only the older boys got large dinners. Rudy had been hungry before. His family had been through hard times as most Navajos had. But someone would always get some money, and butcher a sheep. At St. Michael's, there would *never* be such a feast for the seventh grade boys.

Rudy tried to do well at St. Michael's, but he often slipped and spoke Navajo. When he had gone to public school, boys and girls played together. Sometimes he forgot and spoke a few words to a girl, which he was punished for.

Finding Ways to Save Food

Rudy invented ways to hide food. If something mushy, like baked beans or prunes, was served at breakfast, Rudy would smear it onto a slice of bread. He would then stick it inside his shirt to eat later during chores. The other young boys copied Rudy's shirt sandwiches.

Moving on to Another School

In the summer of 1944, Rudy packed his things. The school had *not* been the right place for him. When he rejoined his family, he told his mother he wanted to go to another school. Disappointed, Adelle discussed this with her other relatives. One of her sisters, nicknamed Cocoa, had heard good things about the Presbyterian Mission School at Ganado. This school taught students from many tribes. Students had to pay to attend. However, during summers they could work to earn their fees.

The decision was made. Rudy would go to Presbyterian Mission School in the fall. All summer Rudy enjoyed looking after his brother and sister. He took them on outings. He even created a snack that became a family favorite. He took pork and beans, put them in dumplings, and cooked them in tomato juice. They were Donna's favorite meal.[2]

In the fall Rudy and his mother got a ride over to Ganado. They entered the gate to the Presbyterian mission. They stood, amazed.[3] There must have been almost fifty buildings!

"This place is a whole town," Rudy thought. He began to feel worried.[4] His father had been gone for years. His mother had always worked, so he had become an independent boy. Yet the size of the mission seemed almost too much for Rudy. He felt lost.

Speaking the Native Language

Rudy was comforted when a nice-looking teenage boy came to talk to him in Navajo. He welcomed Rudy and his mother politely.

Rudy was surprised to hear the boy speak to him in Navajo. He asked if students were allowed to speak the language. The boy assured him that even though classes were taught in English, the students could speak their native languages. The boy gestured for Rudy to follow him. Rudy waved goodbye to his mother. He decided he would give this new school a try.[5]

School and Art — Perfect Together

A wonderful thing happened to Rudy Gorman. He found himself in a school that loved the arts. Ganado had a better school routine. The students did just two hours of morning chores. Then they had classes and study. Rudy never felt overworked at Ganado. Being well fed helped, but being encouraged was food for his spirit.

His English teacher gave him the latest books to read. Rudy read *Spin A Silver Dollar* by Alberta Hannum. This novel was about the Lippincotts. They ran the Wide Ruin Trading Post on the reservation. Beatien Yazz, a Navajo boy, did the illustrations. Rudy was impressed by the young Yazz's paintings.

Dr. Clarence Salsbury, the director of the school, loved all the arts. Students were given music lessons. They were taught to write their

"Yossi-Bah" (1988) is one of Gorman's silk screen prints. Silk screening is a different process than lithography. The image is etched onto porous silk screens using wax. Where the wax hardens, the ink cannot be forced through the screen onto the paper. The encouragement Rudy received at Ganado helped him develop his artistic skills.

own songs. Every Christmas, the school put on a musical pageant. Navajo students, along with Hopis, Lagunas, Apaches, and others sang carols in their own languages. Rudy's paternal grandmother had once translated hymns. He sang them happily in the pageant.[6]

Even chores were not so bad. Rudy drove the mule cart that hauled the trash cans. When work was for the good of the school, and not for punishment, he didn't mind doing it.

Rudy was introduced to a petite woman named Jenny Louis Lind. She volunteered to teach art at the school. She had heard that Rudy liked to draw. It wasn't proper manners to stare at a woman's face openly, so Rudy glanced quickly at Miss Lind. Rudy had seen picture books in the school library. Some books had pictures drawn by Native-American artists. Miss Lind had lots of books. They showed the paintings of artists from all over the world.

Rudy's heart started to pound. Once at a trading post he had seen such paintings. The man said they were made with oil paint.

Soon Rudy would paint with oils. He would also learn to use tempera, watercolors, and pen and ink.

The months flew by. With Miss Lind's help, Rudy did a large collection of charcoal drawings and sketches. He did some oil and tempera paintings. Mostly, he drew in the traditional way of other Native-American artists. He copied their cartoon-like, flat, colorful forms. But his skill grew.

A Working Artist

At the end of Rudy's first year, Miss Lind showed his art to the doctors and nurses who ran the Ganado Mission Hospital. She told them these works were by a very promising student. What did they think?

The doctors and nurses bought Rudolph Carl Gorman's first collection. They paid a dollar or two for each work. At the age of fourteen, he was a working artist.

Rudy spent the summer working at Ganado to pay his school fees.

The End of the War

At the end of the summer, Japan surrendered to the Allies. The war with Japan was over and the Gorman family discovered what their father's secret job had been. Carl Gorman and the other Navajo Code Talkers had radioed information under the noses of the Japanese invaders. Using their native language as a base, they made up a code. For three years, on many South Pacific Islands, they fooled the enemy. No one could break their clever code. The Code Talkers had done much to defeat the Japanese. Some were killed or wounded, but Carl Gorman had survived. Rudy was very proud of his father.

Sadly, Rudy's father would not be returning to live with his mother.[7]

Rudy worked hard during eighth, ninth, and

R.C. Gorman has been a "working artist" since he was fourteen years old. Here, Gorman is working at his easel, blending an oil pastel drawing. A large ceramic vase sits beside him. On this vase, when the clay was still somewhat soft, Gorman drew the image of his model. Her head and hand can be seen resting on her raised knee. Master ceramists will take the vase into their studio. They will lay on the enamel to reveal Gorman's drawing. Then, they will fire the vase in a furnace. The enamel and the clay harden and bond together.

tenth grades at Ganado. He was good at most subjects, especially the arts. He was weak in math. He sometimes found it hard to concentrate. Once he got so distracted playing football that he ran into the goalpost and knocked himself out.

Getting a Summer Job

Rudy's uncle Clarence Gorman was only a year older than Rudy. He said they could get summer jobs at the Bright Angel Lodge at the Grand Canyon. Rudy decided that he would make more money there than at the school. He and Clarence were given jobs as handymen and busboys at the lodge. On the way, Rudy put his best paintings in a folder. He hitched a ride to Gallup, New Mexico. This town was near the Arizona border.

He chose one of the trading posts and went in to offer his work for sale. The white woman looked over Rudy's work and nodded. Rudy did not realize he should have signed some sort of form. He said he'd be back at the end of the summer to see how the paintings sold.

The woman nodded again.

Rudy and Clarence had an interesting summer

working in the restaurant and lodge. Soon it was time for Rudy to return to Ganado. But before he started school, Rudy returned to Gallup. He wanted to find out if any of his art works had sold at the trading post.

Trading Post Problems

The same woman he had met three months before frowned at Rudy when he noticed his paintings were gone. Rudy asked politely for the money she owed him.

"I don't know you," the women replied.

Rudy persisted. His paintings had sold, and he was owed money.

"What money?" said the woman, and she turned away.[8]

Rudy was helpless. Swallowing his fury, he wondered how many others this woman had ignored. Rudy had learned about the kindness of white people like Dr. Salsbury and Jenny Louis Lind, and the others on the staff at Ganado. But he had also met some people who took advantage of Native Americans. He decided that when he got older, no one would steal his money again.

When Rudy Gorman graduated with the

Class of 1950, he was near the top of his class in his grades. He was the author and star of the senior play. He was now ready and eager to take on the outside world.[9] However, he would need to decide exactly where he would go and what he would do.

TAKING ON THE OUTSIDE WORLD

A fter his high school graduation, Rudy Gorman knew he had to decide his future path. His father had been discharged in 1945 from the Marines. He had served throughout the war. Rudy's mother had fallen in love with another man. Carl and Adelle Gorman were divorced. Rudy's father went to study at the Otis Art Institute of Los Angeles. Rudy and his father exchanged letters and visits often.

Going to College

Like his father, Rudy enrolled in college. He went to Arizona State College at Flagstaff. But he kept thinking of the world beyond the American Southwest. After one semester, he became restless. He needed to travel. Gorman decided to join the Navy in 1951. Soon after he completed basic training at San Diego, he visited his father in Los Angeles. Both the sight of the huge "City of Angels" and the Pacific Ocean impressed him.

Gorman would come to know that ocean well. After serving at the Naval Air Station, he got his wish for travel. He spent nearly two years stationed on the South Pacific island of Guam. Carl Gorman and the Navajo Code Talkers had helped free this island from the Japanese in 1944.

In the Navy

Rudy Gorman had met many young people at college. But the young men he met in the Navy were from all over America. They spoke with accents he had never heard before. They came from towns he had never heard of. They had differing religions and family backgrounds. Most of them were unfamiliar with Native Americans.

Gorman had never been fond of the name "Rudolph Carl." He decided he would choose a new name to go with his fresh white uniform. He told his shipmates, such as Bryan Klages from Minnesota and Ronald Rutt from Pennsylvania, that they could call him R.C.[1]

He would be remembered as "Rudy" by his family members, childhood friends, and teachers. But the nickname "R.C." stuck.

While working for the Navy, Gorman found time to take courses in literature and journalism along with Ron Rutt. They went to class at an extension of Ohio State University on Guam. Airmen at the base teased Gorman about studying writing.

Rutt claimed that all Gorman did was draw. He was always practicing, drawing Rutt's hands or face.

The seamen had calendars with drawings of beautiful women by an artist named Petty. Gorman got an idea. The men could give him snapshots of their wives or girlfriends. He would draw their heads. He would then put these drawings on top of a drawing that looked like a beautiful Petty Girl. Of course he'd charge for his work: seven dollars for officers, and two dollars for enlisted men. News of Gorman's skill spread throughout the base. Soon he had more offers than he could handle. He earned his extra money while practicing what he loved most: the drawing of women.

After his two years on Guam, Gorman served on the aircraft carrier *U.S.S. Oriskany*. This ship patrolled the Pacific Coast of the United States. Gorman was discharged in 1955 near San Jose, California. Again, career plans had to be made. At age twenty-four, Gorman returned to Arizona State College at Flagstaff. This time he studied both literature and art.

Back to College

Gorman learned many art forms. But after less than two years, the urge to roam became strong. His family had moved on with their lives. His father was working as an illustrator at Douglas Aircraft and painting in Santa Monica, California. Although he had been divorced for many years, Carl Gorman had not remarried. R.C. Gorman's mother lived in Arizona with Mr. Mitchell. They were raising three children: Shirley, Butch, and Douglas. Gorman's own brother, Don, and sister, Donna, had begun boarding school. In the 1950s, they went to St. Michael's School.[2]

During the summer Gorman took a job at the new Disneyland. It was an amusement park outside Los Angeles. He rowed a canoe and wore a costume. He worked at the Indian Village with many young people. He enjoyed the role and the money.[3]

The Artist's Life

Gorman decided to try the artist's life in San Francisco. He rented a tiny studio and worked odd jobs to survive. San Francisco was a huge city. At first he felt alone. Soon, though, Gorman got to know many painters, poets, actors, and models. He absorbed their ideas and styles.

Once he played basketball on a playground in his neighborhood. There he made friends with a college student named Myrsan Wixman. During the winter, Wixman's father sent money for his son to visit him at home in Mexico. Wixman decided Gorman should come along.

Gorman and Wixman arrived in Guadalajara. Gorman had studied the great European painters in books. But he had not studied the fine

Mexican painters working durng the 1930s and 1940s. He noticed an institute for orphans in Guadalajara. There he found some murals by the late José Clemente Orozco. Orozco's paintings were very large. He did the figures of simple Mexican people. He showed them working the fields, grinding corn, and living the life of the earth. To see these murals took Gorman's breath away. Someone painted native people like *his* people, the Navajos of his youth. It excited him that this artist had been paid for painting these subjects![4]

Mexican Artists

Gorman and Wixman traveled on to Mexico City. There they saw important works by Mexican artists like Diego Rivera, David Siqueiros, and Rufino Tamayo.[5] These works showed that it was important for an artist to draw on the images of his own culture. Soon Gorman and Wixman headed back to California. Gorman believed that somehow he would return to Mexico to study art.

Gorman visited his father for advice and help. He also wanted to get to know his stepmother Mary Wilson. She had married Carl after many years of being his friend and supporter. Their son

Alfred Kee was born in April 1957. Gorman had a new half-brother to enjoy. It was during this summer visit that Gorman said he needed funds in order to study art in Mexico City. His father helped him apply. In 1958, Gorman's dream came true. He was given money from the tribe for school.

Gorman took classes at Mexico City College that stressed the importance of using models for art. "Michael's Lady" is one of Gorman's oil pastel drawings. To start, Gorman prepares his easel in his studio. He then poses his model. Next, he roughs out the drawing on heavy paper using colored sticks of oil pastel. He dips brushes into a paint thinner. He blends the colors of the model, her clothes, and her background.

Spanish Refresher Course

Gorman struggled to improve his Spanish so he could talk to his host Mexican family and his teachers. Mexico City College stressed life drawing and all basic skills. Once at Chinle School Gorman was spanked for drawing a nude woman. Now he was taught to draw figures every day. Professional models posed for classes. They were well paid. Gorman stored the idea of posing away in his head.

An American girl, Beth Brenneman, was in Mexico perfecting her Spanish. She became one of Gorman's best friends. He took her to college, where she was hired as a model. Together with other art students, they explored the ancient pyramids. They shared simple picnics of cheese, bread, and wine. They even joined the Mexicans and cheered at bullfights.

While working in Mexico, Gorman became like the Mexican painters he admired. He began to draw upon the subjects and landscapes he carried within his heart.

San Francisco in 1960 was a lively arts center. Artists painted in oil and with acrylics. Some worked in watercolors. Some did clay sculptures. Others drew with charcoal and china markers. Young poets read their unusual work in coffeehouses. Folk musicians sang beside them. Gorman returned to San Francisco to join this crowd. He worked night shifts at the post office to earn money. He drew and painted all day.

He slept only a few hours a night. Luckily, he had a lot of energy.

Gorman remembered that modeling was hard work but that it paid well. He decided he would try it. He'd always admired the human body. He was not embarrassed to have his used for the sake of art. Soon he was hired to model for university classes. He also modeled for private art groups, both with and without his clothes. While modeling, he heard the teachers lecture and criticize works. He learned while he earned.

Life in Texas

During the next year, Gorman also briefly tried life in Houston, Texas. He became close friends with artist Barry Tinkler and builder Clifton Klotz. Tracy Evans became both a friend and a model for Gorman. But the city of San Francisco pulled him back.

At last, Gorman had enough good work to get some galleries to see him. By 1963 two city galleries gave him shows. His work made a hit with the public.

Moving on to New Mexico

Once again, R.C. Gorman felt the urge to travel. He returned to the site of his childhood ceremonials, Gallup, New Mexico. There he met his friend Barry Tinkler from Houston. They enjoyed the Native-American crafts and dancing. Then they took a bus over to Taos. This small New Mexican town was already famous for its galleries. Gorman brought slides of some of his paintings, hoping a gallery owner might look at them and become interested in his work.

Gorman and Tinkler arrived at night, and found a motel. Gorman awoke to see a ring of majestic mountains rising up beyond the village. Down the road was the Taos Pueblo. It was the oldest Native-American settlement in America which still actively housed its tribe. Gorman loved the town.

A gallery owner named John Manchester looked over the slides that Gorman showed him. Many of these paintings were based on Native-American themes, but they were unusual and modern. Manchester said after studying only a few slides that he would buy them all! In fact, Manchester said that if Gorman would send him some paintings and let him get interest going, he could promise him a one-man show during September of the following year.[6]

R.C. Gorman was pleased. Very few galleries in the southwest showed paintings by Native Americans. Manchester's enthusiasm was a breakthrough for the artist.

As Gorman left Taos to go back to San Francisco, he turned and gazed at the great, snow-tipped Sangre de Cristo Mountains. They towered over the Rio Grande Valley. A seed was planted in his mind.

Not only would Gorman return to Taos for his one-man show, perhaps he would return someday to make Taos his home.[7]

6

MASTERING HIS CRAFT

In October 1964, R.C. Gorman traveled to Tulsa, Oklahoma, to meet his father. The Philbrook Museum was giving them their first art show together. It was called "New Directions in American Indian Art."[1] Carl Gorman had ten works in oil, casein, and watercolor. R.C. had thirteen works in oil, oil pastel, and linoleum block print. This exhibit was a high point for both Carl and R.C. Gorman as artists and as family. Curator Jeanne Snodgrass hosted an opening night party for Carl's fifty-seventh birthday. At this event, father and son could show their pleasure and pride in each other.

R.C. Gorman, in his early thirties, stands beside an oil portrait he painted of his father, Carl Gorman. R.C. and Carl Gorman had their first joint shows in 1964 and 1965. R.C. showed this painting there.

Father and Son Art Show

Carl Gorman was asked why he did not paint in the traditional Native-American way. He replied that life for the Navajo was harsh and cruel, a constant battle with nature. "Having grown up in Navajo country," he said, "I am keenly aware of this and try to bring out some of this feeling . . ."[2]

R.C. agreed. The old ways of painting Native-American subjects were not right for him. He wanted to try many different styles and media to express himself as an artist.

In 1965, R.C. and Carl Gorman had another successful father-and-son show. This one was in Phoenix, Arizona, at the Heard Museum. At this show, R.C. was asked if he had objections to being teamed up with his father. He laughed and replied: "None whatsoever! I need all the promotion I can get."[3]

Another artist was growing up: R.C.'s little half-brother "Kee." Kee loved to draw and paint almost from infancy. By age seven Kee had won first place in the Scottsdale Indian Art exhibit for juveniles. R.C., a winner of many Indian art awards, was delighted. When visiting Carl and Mary's southern California home, he watched Kee paint. He told Carl: "That boy is great. . . .You'll see, Dad, he'll be better than all of us."[4]

Soon Kee was winning more awards and starting to sell his work. John Manchester's Gallery in Taos was making R.C. Gorman into a well-known painter in the southwest. This gallery also showed Kee's paintings. Two of them sold, and Manchester asked for more.

A One-Man Show

In September 1965, R.C. Gorman had a one-man show at the Manchester Gallery. His mother Adelle, his Aunt Mary, and Carl and Mary Gorman were all there. They wore colorful Navajo shirts and silver jewelry. Friends from the Taos Pueblo performed native dances. White and Native-American people mingled and joined in the Friendship Dance.

Manchester said after this exciting show. "It was almost like a new beginning, a revolution . . ."[5] No serious gallery in the southwest had opened up like this to a modern Native-American painter. R.C. Gorman had started a whole new field.

By 1966 Gorman had more shows in Phoenix and San Francisco galleries. When his mother, Adelle, saw his paintings hanging, she said to him, "I never dreamed this is how you would make a living. Or I would have encouraged you more."[6]

That summer of 1966 Gorman lived on top of one of San Francisco's steep hills. He had to climb up twenty flights of stairs to get to his studio. Many important people had discovered his work. Other Native-American artists came to him. Together they formed the American Indian

Artists group. Gorman helped the others in getting their work shown.

Gorman not only drew and painted Native-American women. He did a series of paintings of geometric designs from Navajo rugs and pottery. He also painted the *yei* figures from the Navajo religious ceremonies.

During a trip to the Art Wagon Gallery in Phoenix, Arizona, Gorman met Raul Anguiano, a Mexican artist who worked in lithography. After talking to Gorman, Señor Anguiano said that most of the great Mexican artists drew their lithographs at

R.C. Gorman calls this lithograph "First Choice." He means that the lady has made her first choice of blankets. Women on both sides of his family wove patterned wool blankets.

the printing studio of Señor José Sanchez. With Gorman's skill in drawing, he might work well in lithography.

R.C. Gorman did not know much about this

kind of art, but he trusted Señor Anguiano. He promised to come down in the fall to Mexico City, where Anguiano would introduce him to Sanchez.[7] Again, Gorman would have to struggle with his Spanish.

Tragedy Strikes

One day in August, R.C. received terrible news. Carl, Mary, their baby daughter Zonnie, Kee, and Mary's mother, Mrs. Wilson, had all been traveling from their family home in Arizona toward Albuquerque, New Mexico. Mary, the driver, lost control. The van rolled, throwing the entire family out. By the time the ambulances got them all to the nearest hospital in Grants, New Mexico, Mary and Zonnie were unconscious with concussions. Carl was critically wounded. He had a shattered pelvis. Mrs. Wilson died in two days. Kee Gorman was dead on arrival.

R.C. Gorman had no car. He never learned to drive. But he got to New Mexico as fast as he could. By the time he arrived, Mary and Zonnie were out of danger. Carl was a physically powerful man for his age. He would live. But how would the family survive the loss of their beloved little boy? Mary told R.C. that even in her grief she had to go on to care for Zonnie and Carl. The doctors had told her privately that Carl might not walk again, but they decided never to tell him that. Mary believed if Carl's spirit could heal without his son Kee, he would heal despite what the doctors said.

R.C. stayed in a motel in Grants. He helped Mary and Zonnie and spoke to his father each day in the hospital. But Carl's depression could not be cured by words. Carl said he could never paint again. R.C. felt helpless. The only way he could completely express his pain for his father's loss was to draw. A portrait of Carl and other drawings of grieving people helped R.C. get through this rough time.[8]

When Gorman finally saw that his father would fight to walk again, he returned to San Francisco. But anger and sadness found their way into his work for a long time after that summer. The painful image of a young brother who would never know the joy of a life in art stayed with him forever.

R.C. Gorman continued to work. The trip to Mexico City to learn lithography worked out well. Señor Sanchez was an experienced printer.

By using key words in Spanish, he taught Gorman the skills of drawing on polished stone slabs with a grease pencil. Gorman soon found he was a natural for this art form. His drawing could be printed many times using colored inks. This process would give hundreds of people the chance to own an image of his that only one person could own before.

In 1968 the Navajo tribe celebrated the one-hundredth anniversary of their return to their Arizona homeland following The Long Walk. The Long Walk was a forced roundup and march of the tribe from their northern Arizona homeland to Fort Sumner. This fort was 180 miles southeast of Santa Fe, New Mexico. The Army did this to control the Navajo. Those who survived the four-year imprisonment (only about one-quarter of those who were sent away) were marched home to a reservation.[9] One of them was Peshlakai, R.C. Gorman's great-grandfather.

A Tribute to "The Long Walk"

To mark this homecoming of his tribe, R.C. Gorman did a series of "Long Walk" drawings. The Navajos in them were weary, sad, starved, and barefoot. But they were survivors.

Gorman was still in search of a homeland himself. He had many wonderful friends, fellow artists and models in San Francisco, but he did not feel "rooted." Something about Taos, New Mexico, kept calling to him. Taos was not on the Navajo reservation. It was not within the actual borders of the tribe's Four Sacred Mountains. Traditional Navajos believe that these mountains bound the land given them by their gods. Still, the town drew Gorman back.

While visiting Taos that summer, R.C. Gorman talked to John Manchester. Manchester wanted to sell his gallery. They discussed what kind of deal they might make. The old two-story adobe building down the unpaved road was hard to find. It needed many repairs. Still, Gorman wanted it. His father agreed to loan him part of the down payment. The bankers in Taos finally lent him the rest of the money he needed.

Running His Own Gallery

In the autumn of 1968, Gorman became the first Native-American artist to run his own fine-art gallery. He knew he'd have to actually live and work in the gallery. He would need to invest every dollar he made in the place, but he did not care. He stood in front of the building and hung its new sign, "The Navajo Gallery." He then looked up at the golden trees covering the hills. He grinned at the blue sky behind the snow-tipped peak of Taos Mountain. He had made a homecoming.

During the early days at the gallery, Gorman's friends came and helped him. He couldn't pay them. They did it because his joy was catching! His friend from Houston, builder Clifton Klotz, came out to help remodel the building. A Navajo friend, Ella Natonabah, had secretarial skills. She typed and kept the records. She also welcomed any customers. Gorman and Natonabah talked in Navajo as they prepared native foods. Native-American artist friends convinced Gorman to show their work. In return, they promoted him to all the competitions and galleries around the country.

At the end of the 1960s, Gorman again entered the Scottsdale Indian Arts Exhibition. This time his Navajo rug painting took first prize, a drawing took second prize, and an abstract oil took third prize. Now there wasn't a single collector in the country who did not know the name R.C. Gorman.

R.C. Gorman does business in the studio at his home in El Prado, New Mexico. Although he is best at being an artist, when Gorman opened his gallery he was forced to become a businessman as well.

News of the Navajo Gallery spread like wildfire. The tribe's own newspaper, *The Navajo Times*, wrote articles about R.C. Gorman. Patrons wanted more of his work. He drew in his living room-studio all morning with a live model and opened the gallery after lunch. Sales increased greatly during this time.

Gorman was kept busy running to framing shops, buying supplies, taking phone calls, and doing business. He was also shipping as much work as possible to other galleries. He needed more staff, yet he couldn't afford anyone else. Eventually a young man was hired to keep the house in good repair and to stretch the canvases for painting. Gorman left the gallery accounting and taxes to bookkeepers. Soon he found that these bookkeepers were cheating him. They were taking his money and *not* paying his taxes.

Gorman remembered the time when the Gallup trading post owner had sold his paintings and cheated him. He had vowed it would not happen again, but he was an artist, not a businessman. He wanted to make people happy and please them instead of distrusting them. He wanted to save his best energy for his art, not for managing the business.

Each day R.C. Gorman felt what he called "the magic of Taos." However, if he did not get a team of good workers, the Navajo Gallery might not survive.

GORMAN GOES
INTERNATIONAL

Help for R.C. Gorman was about to arrive. One day in the summer of 1978, Gorman was standing at his easel, finishing a painting. His model had left. He was trying to run the gallery and paint at the same time. Phones kept ringing and customers wandered in and out of the gallery. The weather was hot. He wore a folded bandana headband, sign of the unmarried Navajo male. It was also very practical for working. He wore a loose shirt that hung over his jeans.

Through the front windows Gorman saw a young woman walk down the path to his door. "Hey, Sally Sandwich!" he called to her.

Gorman had suggested that his good friend Virginia Dooley become "Sally Sandwich" for a summer job. She would sell gallery staffers around town a fresh sandwich each day. At first Dooley felt a little foolish about Gorman's nickname. He also insisted she wear a decorated bonnet! She soon learned, however, that everything Gorman did for publicity usually resulted in profit.[1]

During her first year as a music teacher for the Taos Elementary Schools, Virginia Dooley had become close friends with R.C. Gorman. In 1969, she had taught high-school music on the Navajo reservation. She learned much about the ways of Navajo people.[2] When she arrived in Taos, Dooley was eager to meet R.C. Gorman. She had gotten to know his father. Carl had given lectures on Navajo culture near where she was teaching.

"When you opened your gallery," she told Gorman, "everybody up on the reservation thought it was fantastic." Her Navajo students who studied art hoped to someday be good enough to show at the Navajo Gallery. Gorman had become a kind of hero to them.

Gorman and Dooley Working Together

Gorman and Dooley got along right away. Gorman wanted his gallery to survive. It was a business he loved. Also, he wanted to inspire future artists like those students. So he asked Dooley if she'd like to try working at the Navajo Gallery. She could just work evenings and weekends when she was not teaching school. Dooley had no business training, but she had a natural talent for organization and dealing with people. She decided to give it a try.

Running the gallery was a challenge. Coping with Gorman, his models, his customers, photographers, relatives, friends, and various household pets kept Dooley busy. She learned the business quickly. Gorman asked her to take a full-time position.

At first she was reluctant. Music was the career for which she had studied. "Don't worry," Gorman told her. "The main thing I need is someone who doesn't go to lunch!" Dooley also wondered if one should work for a friend. Would it be awkward?[3] She decided to leave teaching and work full-time. By 1972, Dooley became the gallery director.

Dooley allowed Gorman to expand his sales

while he traveled and did lithographs. Someone was still needed to prepare canvases, ship work, and go to a gallery showing Gorman's art. Curtis Grubbs came through Taos looking for a mutual friend. Gorman asked if he'd like to join the staff. Grubbs agreed to be the studio assistant and road manager for Gorman. Soon Dooley and Grubbs formed a team. They freed Gorman from business dealings so he was able to work only on his art.

Also in those early years, Gorman wanted the Navajo Gallery to host shows for other Native-American artists. Eventually, though, Gorman found he did best selling only his own work. He liked appearing at shows and being photographed and quoted. He had a natural fondness for jokes and clowning. He began using a fancier version of his work clothes as his "trademark outfit." He wore a colorful fabric bandana folded into a headband and dressy, long shirt over tailored slacks.

Gorman's Career Takes Off

During his forties, Gorman's career hit its full stride, partly because of his "home team": Dooley and Grubbs, soon joined by secretary-bookkeeper

Rosalie Talbott. He also had found a new group of coworkers: master printers. In 1971-72, Gorman did a group of lithographs called "Homage to Navajo Women" at the Tamarind Institute. It caused a sensation. He then produced a series of six nude drawings he called "Bodies by Gorman." These were the first nudes put out by a Native-American artist.

Lithography meant that each one of Gorman's drawings could be perfectly reproduced many times, but it was an expensive art form. It cost money up front. He needed a partner to share the costs.[4] He found one in Byron Butler, a doctor from Phoenix. Butler and his wife were early collectors from Gorman's San Francisco shows. With the Butlers, he formed *Art Consultants Ltd.* This allowed him to move into the medium that he would come to love most.[5]

Gorman never married. Most of his relatives, except for young Zonnie, had already produced families of their own. His extended family welcomed Gorman's love and assistance. As his finances improved, he helped young relatives with school, lessons, and travel. His gallery home housed pet dogs, fish, and cats. In the early 1970s, he also had an iguana, a defumed skunk, and, for a while, a pet pig. The iguana and the skunk were eventually given to the Albuquerque Zoo, mainly because they frightened his models. The pig disappeared suspiciously before a large barbeque party was held down the road.

More Family Losses

By 1972, Gorman's father had recovered his strength and was teaching at the University of California in Davis. Then Gorman received another shock. His mother's youngest son, Douglas, died of heart failure. In 1973, his mother also passed away. Gorman was stunned to lose both his half-brother and his beloved mother in so short a time. Referring to his mother as his first love, Gorman said of her: ". . . she was my guiding light. I only wish I could have shown her more of the world."[6]

Gorman found he was happiest drawing women, in oil pastel or on the lithostone. He attracted wonderful models. He let his models feel free. They could bring their babies, rearrange their hair, or wear shawls or blankets. Gorman looked for variety in women, in their size, mood, and spirit. He especially liked their nice bare feet! Most women who posed for him were mixed race, Hispanic, or Asian. Only his niece Miriam Gorman, and his cousin Grace Davis, who both posed for him, were full-blooded Navajo.

Finding Models to Pose

Gorman found his models everywhere. Bernadette Track, half Taos Pueblo and half Lakota, became a Gorman model for sixteen years. A trained dancer, Track inspired him with her grace. Taosena Laila Bynoe had six children. Gorman drew Bynoe with each baby over the years. Bynoe spent so much time posing for Gorman that he joked: "I'm practically her second husband."[7]

Many people told Gorman that an Anglo waitress, Mary Lou Stewart, looked like "a Gorman woman." Gorman asked her to come to his studio and pose. Happily, she did so.[8]

Gorman's Native-American women are representative of every woman.

Gorman kept up such a hectic pace that even his amazing energy was drained. He did monthly gallery shows. He worked in his studio, producing many drawings. He did lithographs at four different presses. A film crew from KAET-TV took over Gorman's life to make a documentary on him for Public Television.

Gorman admitted that the work had become his life. His frequent model and printer with Richard Newlin, Yoko Saito, said of him: "Gorman has an insatiable appetite and capacity for working, working, working."[9]

By the end of the 1970s, more of Gorman's dreams had come true. He had taken courses at colleges in Flagstaff, Mexico City, Guam, and San Francisco. He had never, however, gotten a four-year degree. His *alma mater*, Presbyterian Mission High School, had now expanded into the College of Ganado, Arizona. In 1978, this college awarded him an honorary doctorate of fine arts. Also, on January 8, 1979, the governor of New Mexico declared it to be R.C. Gorman Day.

Although Gorman had been included in books about Native-American artists, a book was published in 1978 that was only about him and his lithographs. Gorman had loved books all his life, but he could never afford to buy them until adulthood. For this reason, the success of this book deeply moved him. Eventually, other books about his posters, drawings, and complete graphics would also be published.

MUSÉE MUNICIPAL DE SAINT-PAUL

R.C. GORMAN

du 9 Mai au 4 Juin 1979

▽

Gorman has used many of his drawings for posters. A poster is a fine photographic representation. But it is not limited like a lithograph or silk screen. More copies can be made. However, some of Gorman's posters were used for special purposes. Now many of these have gone out of print.

By the end of the decade, R.C. Gorman had held one-man shows all over America. He had branched out into clay sculpture. Working in clay reminded him of the day when he knelt in the mud and created figures to use as toys. One of his first efforts was a bust of his father.

A Tribute to Carl Gorman

This sculpture, when bronzed, gave a powerful image of Carl Gorman at age seventy. His profile was still strong, face unwrinkled, and his gray hair was tied back in the Navajo style knotted with white yarn. A wonderful evening was shared by R.C., Carl, and their family when this sculpture was unveiled for the public in a San Francisco art gallery. The title of the sculpture was: "Portrait of a Navajo Code Talker."

By 1978, Gorman had noticed that many potential art buyers never made it up to Taos, but did pass through the historic district of Albuquerque called Old Town. He decided that Old Town would be a good place for a second gallery. He achieved another first and became the owner of two galleries. The Navajo Gallery in Old Town was a success from the start.[10]

Having his personal living space be part of his gallery had become impractical for Gorman. He had no room to work on more than one easel at a time. He had little storage space, no sculpture space, and no privacy. He needed wall space to hang his growing art collection. He also wanted more room to entertain his visiting relatives.

Soon he found an old, walled hacienda on a hill north of Taos. It stood directly at the foot of his beloved mountains in the village of El Prado. The main rooms were over two hundred years old. Gorman fell in love with the site. Architects showed him how to enlarge it into a comfortable house and studio. By the end of the decade, Gorman moved into the first private home that he had ever owned.

The hacienda on the hill (fondly referred to as Fort Gorman by many locals) was expanded during the early 1980s. Gorman added rooms, an indoor pool, sculpture gardens, and two guest houses. Now he needed one more member on his team: an expert housekeeper. He found one in Rose Roybal, who capably oversees the food service, grounds staff, and social schedule of the entire estate.

R.C. Gorman stands in his sculpture courtyard with two of his larger-than-life bronzes, "Nellie Begay" and "Natoma."

Once young Rudy Gorman's world had been surrounded by two canyons on the Navajo reservation. Now he realized the world of art had no boundary. In 1979, he went international with his show at the Musée Municipal, St. Paul de Vence, France. During the 1980s, he would expand into West Germany and Japan.[11] The joy of international travel became one he would share with his staff members and relatives.

A Navajo song translates: "I seem to be working and thinking, but I am really running through a meadow."[12]

On the wings of his art, Rudy Gorman's meadow had become the entire world.

CHRONOLOGY

1931—July 31, Rudolph Carl Gorman is born in a Chinle, Arizona, hospital to Adelle and Carl.

1937—Donald Gorman is born. Rudy Gorman starts at Chinle Public School, age six.

1939—Donna Gorman is born.

1941—Rudy and Carl Gorman spend the summer working at Kaibito. In December, Japanese bomb Pearl Harbor.

1942—Winter, Carl Gorman enlists in special Marine unit, the Navajo Code Talkers. Adelle Gorman moves the children to the ordnance at Bellemont, Arizona.

1943—German prisoners join the Navajo and Hopi workers at Bellemont In the fall, Gorman starts seventh grade at St. Michael's Mission School for Navajos.

1944—Fall, Gorman begins Ganado Presbyterian Mission High School in Ganado, Arizona.

1945—Summer, Japanese surrender. Navajo Code Talkers are discharged. Carl and Adelle Gorman are divorced.

1949—Summer, Gorman and his young uncle Clarence Gorman work at the Bright Angel Lodge, Grand Canyon, Arizona.

1950—Spring, Gorman graduates from Ganado Presbyterian Mission High School. In the fall, Gorman enrolls at Arizona State College in Flagstaff.

1951—Gorman joins the Navy, receives basic training in San Diego. He serves in the Pacific and Guam. Now called R.C., he studies literature while in Guam.

1955—Gorman is discharged from the Navy at San Jose. He has visited San Francisco and likes the city. Donna and Don Gorman are in boarding school at St. Michael's. Adelle Gorman has a second family with Mr. Mitchell and lives outside Flagstaff. Gorman enrolls again at Arizona State, studying art and literature.

1956—Summer, Gorman works at the new Disneyland in Anaheim, California.

1956-7—Gorman moves to San Francisco to try life as an artist. Carl Gorman marries Mary Wilson and studies art in California.

1957—Gorman accompanies a friend on a family visit to Guadalajara and Mexico City.

1958—Gorman receives a scholarship, awarded by the Navajo Tribe, to study at Mexico City College for a term.

1959—Gorman works between San Francisco and the reservation. He earns money to support his art studies by modeling for classes and working at the post office.

1963—Gorman has his first show in a San Francisco gallery.

1964—R.C. and Carl Gorman have their first joint show at the Philbrook Museum and Art Center in Tulsa, Oklahoma. Later, Gorman and a friend visit Gallup, New Mexico, and for the first time, Taos, New Mexico.

1965—Gorman has a one-man show at the Manchester Gallery in Taos, and considers moving there. Many Gorman family members attend the show.

1966—Gorman continues drawing and painting in his San Francisco studio and has a show in Phoenix. He meets Raul Anguiano who suggests they meet in Mexico and try producing a lithograph. In August, a car accident kills half-brother Kee and injures Carl severely. Stepmother Mary and baby Zonnie recover.

1967—Gorman makes trip to Mexico and produces several lithographs.

1968—Gorman does a series of survivor drawings to commemorate the one-hundredth anniversary of The Long Walk, the forced imprisonment of the Navajos. In the summer, Gorman goes to Taos to discuss buying the gallery. In the fall, Gorman receives financing, moves to Taos, and becomes the first Native-American artist to own his own art gallery.

1969-70—Gorman wins major competitions and shows in many famous galleries. He opens The Navajo Gallery as owner, salesman, and lead artist.

1970—Virginia Dooley, a Taos music teacher,

starts working part-time, running the gallery evenings and weekends.

1972—Virginia Dooley becomes full-time director of the Navajo Gallery. Gorman does his first major lithograph suite, "Homage to Women" at the Tamarind Institute, University of New Mexico. Gorman produces his landmark series of six nudes, "Bodies by Gorman." Gorman's half-brother, Douglas Mitchell, dies of heart failure.

1973—Gorman's mother Adelle dies.

1976—Public Television documentary series called *American Indian Artists* features Gorman in one of their six films.

1978—Gorman's high school, now expanded into College of Ganado, Arizona, awards him an honorary doctorate of fine arts.

1979—January 8 is declared R.C. Gorman Day in the state of New Mexico. Gorman moves to his home in El Prado. Gorman branches out into clay sculpture, imaged ceramics, and pressed paper images in San Francisco.

1980s—Gorman produces lithographs in France and Germany and does wood-cuts in Japan. Gorman receives honorary doctorates from Eastern New Mexico University and Northern Arizona State University.

1986—Gorman receives the Humanitarian Award for American art and intercultural relations at Harvard University.

1988—Gorman receives the New Mexico Governors Award.

1990—Gorman is awarded an honorary doctor of letters degree from Northern Arizona University in Flagstaff, where he was a student in the 1950s.

1993—The American Association of State Colleges and Universities presents Gorman with the Alumnus of the Year Award. His fellow nominee is journalist Dan Rather.

1995—Gorman receives the New Mexico Hispanic Chamber of Commerce Award. This is a great honor since Gorman is not Hispanic.

CHAPTER NOTES

Chapter 1

1. Photo caption, *The Harvard Gazette*, May 2, 1986.

2. The Harvard Foundation for Intercultural and Race Relations. Letter from Dr. S. Allen Counter, March 3, 1986.

3. From "R.C. Gorman's Remarks to Harvard University," May 5, 1986. Courtesy of the Navajo Gallery, Virginia Dooley, director.

4. Ibid.

Chapter 2

1. Virginia Dooley, *R.C. Gorman: Chinle to Taos* (Taos: Navajo Gallery, 1988), pp. 10-11.

2. Interview with Donna Gorman Scott, June 1994.

3. R.C. Gorman, *The Radiance of My People* (Albuquerque: Santa Fe Fine Arts, Inc., 1992), p. 12.

4. Manuscript notes by R.C. Gorman, April 1994.

5. Ibid.

6. Doris Monthan, *R.C. Gorman: The Lithographs* (Flagstaff: Northland Press, 1978), p. 8.; Gorman, *Radiance*, p. 19.

7. Gorman, *Radiance,* p. 19.

8. Interview with R.C. Gorman, June 1994.

9. Monthan, p. 9.

Chapter 3

1. R.C. Gorman, *The Radiance of My People* (Albuquerque: Santa Fe Fine Arts, Inc., 1992), p. 16.

2. Doris Monthan, *R.C. Gorman: The Lithographs* (Flagstaff: Northland Press, 1978), p. 9.

3. "American Indian Artists: R.C. Gorman." A film in the *American Indian Artists Series*, produced by KAET-TV Phoenix, for the Public Broadcasting System, 1976.

4. Monthan, p. 8.

5. Interview with Donna Gorman Scott, June 1994.

6. Henry and Georgia Greenberg, *Carl Gorman World* (Albuquerque: University of New Mexico Press, 1984), p. 48.

7. Ibid., p. 50.

8. Ibid., p. 53.

9. Nathan Aaseng, *Navajo Code Talkers* (New York: Walker & Co., 1992), pp. 25-27.

10. Interview with R.C. Gorman, June 1994.

11. Ibid.

12. Interview with Donna Gorman Scott, June 1994.

13. Ibid.

14. Ibid.

15. Greenberg, p. 63.

Chapter 4

1. Interview with R.C. Gorman, June 1994.

2. Interview with Donna Gorman Scott, June 1994.

3. Jerry McLain, "Dr. Big—A Visit to Ganado's Presbyterian Mission," *Arizona Highways*, August 1948, pp. 4-9.

4. Doris Monthan, *R.C. Gorman: The Lithographs* (Flagstaff: Northland Press, 1978), pp. 10-11.

5. Gorman, p. 21.; Monthan, p. 10.

6. Interview with R.C. Gorman.

7. Ibid.

8. Monthan, p. 13.

9. Ibid., pp. 13-14.

Chapter 5

1. R.C. Gorman, *The Radiance of My People* (Albuquerque: Santa Fe Fine Arts, Inc., 1992), p. 24.

2. Interview with Donna Gorman Scott, June 1994.

3. Gorman, p. 26.

4. Ibid.

5. Virginia Stewart, *45 Contemporary Mexican Artists: A Twentieth-Century Renaissance* (Stanford: Stanford University Press, 1951), pp. 27-30, 56-60, 68-71.

6. Doris Monthan, *R.C. Gorman: The Lithographs* (Flagstaff: Northland Press, 1978), pp. 19-20.

7. Interview with R.C. Gorman, June 1994.

Chapter 6

1. Henry and Georgia Greenberg, *Carl Gorman's World* (Albuquerque: University of New Mexico Press, 1984), p. 83.

2. Ibid., p. 84.

3. Ibid., p. 85.

4. Ibid., p. 104.

5. Doris Monthan, *R.C. Gorman: The Lithographs* (Flagstaff: Northland Press, 1978), p. 20.

6. Ibid.

7. R.C. Gorman, *The Radiance of My People* (Albuquerque: Santa Fe Fine Arts, Inc., 1992), p. 38.

8. Greenberg, pp. 121-122.

9. Clyde Kluckhohn and Dorothea Leighton, *The Navaho* (Cambridge: Harvard University Press, 1948), pp. 8-10.

Chapter 7

1. Interview with Virginia Dooley, June 1994.

2. Ibid.

3. Ibid.

4. Interview with R.C. Gorman, June 1994.

5. R.C. Gorman, *The Radiance of My People* (Albuquerque: Santa Fe Fine Arts Inc., 1992), pp. 49-51.

6. Ibid., p. 46.

7. Mary Beth Green, *R.C. Gorman: The Drawings* (Flagstaff; Northland Press, 1982), p. 21.

8. Virginia Dooley, ed., *Nudes and Foods: Gorman Goes Gourmet* (Flagstaff: Northland Press, 1981), pp. 47-48.

9. Green, p. 19.

10. Interview with Barbara Castner, June 1994.

11. Virginia Dooley. *R.C. Gorman: Chinle to Taos* (Taos: Navajo Gallery, 1988), p. 60.

12. Ibid., p. 2.

BIBLIOGRAPHY

Aaseng, Nathan. *Navajo Code Talkers*. New York: Walker & Co., 1992.

"American Indian Artists: R.C. Gorman." A Film in the *American Indian Artists Series*. Produced by KAET-Phoenix for the Public Broadcasting System, 1976.

Baldwin, Gordon C. *Indians of the Southwest*. New York: G.P. Putnam's Sons, 1970.

Dooley, Virginia, ed. *R.C. Gorman: Chinle to Taos*. Taos: Navajo Gallery, 1988.

Gorman, R.C. *The Radiance of My People*. Albuquerque: Santa Fe Fine Arts Inc., 1992.

Green, Mary Beth. *R.C. Gorman: The Drawings*. Flagstaff: Northland Press, 1982.

Greenberg, Henry and Georgia. *Carl Gorman's World*. Albuquerque: University of New Mexico Press, 1984.

Hannum, Alberta. *Spin A Silver Dollar*. (With Paintings in Full Color by Beatien Yazz.) New York: Viking Press, 1945, reprinted 1961.

Henningsen, Chuck, and Stephen Parks. *R.C. Gorman: A Portrait.* Boston: Little, Brown & Co., 1983.

Hurst, Tricia. *R.C. Gorman: The Posters.* Flagstaff: Northland Press, 1980.

Kluckhohn, Clyde, and Dorothea Leighton. *The Navaho.* Cambridge: Harvard University Press, 1948.

LaFarge, Oliver. *As Long as the Grass Shall Grow.* New York and Toronto: Longmans, Green and Company; Alliance Book Corporation, 1940.

McLain, Jerry. "Dr. Big—A Visit to Ganado's Presbyterian Mission." *Arizona Highways,* August 1948.

Monthan, Doris. *R.C. Gorman: The Lithographs.* Flagstaff: Northland Press, 1978.

Monthan, Guy and Doris. *Art and Indian Individualists: The Art of Seventeen Contemporary Southwestern Artists and Craftsmen.* Flagstaff: Northland Press, 1975.

Nelson, Mary Carroll. "R.C. Gorman: Navajo in Vogue." *American Artist,* September 1974.

Newcomb, Franc Johnson. *Navajo Neighbors.* Norman: University of Oklahoma Press, 1966.

New Mexico. Compiled by Workers of the Writers' Program, W.P.A. in the State of New Mexico. Albuquerque: University of New Mexico Press, 2nd ed., 1945.

Oakes, Maud. *Where the Two Came to Their Father— A Navajo War Ceremonial.* Commentary by Joseph Campbell. Princeton: Princeton University Press, Bollingen Series I, paperback ed., 1991.

Parks, Stephen. "R.C. Gorman: Changing Man." *Southwest Profile*, July 1988.

Rosen, Kenneth, ed. *The Man to Send Rain Clouds: Contemporary Stories by American Indians.* illus. by R.C. Gorman and Aaron Yava. New York: Viking Press, 1974.

Smart, Ted, and David Gibbon. *Grand Canyon: Arizona and New Mexico.* New York: Crescent Books, 1979.

Smith, Dama Margaret. *Indian Tribes of the Southwest.* Stanford: Stanford University Press, 1933.

Somerville, Donald. *World War II Day by Day. An Illustrated Almanac 1939-1945.* Greenwich,

CT.: Dorset Press of the Brompton Books Corporation, 1989.

Stewart, Virginia. *45 Contemporary Mexican Artists: A Twentieth-Century Renaissance.* Stanford: Stanford University Press, 1951.

INDEX